CLOUD VAPING

The 4 Generations of Electronic
Cigarettes Explained

What's Good and What's Not

By

Shane Alexander

Published by:

CSB Academy Publishing Company.
P.O. Box 966
Semmes, Alabama 36575

Cover & Interior designed
By
Angie Anderson

First Edition

TABLE OF CONTENTS

1. INTRODUCTION

In the world of ever changing and fast pace e-cigarettes, new changes are coming from both the government and from the e-cigarette manufacturers. How does anyone keep up with all these changes? I have been in the e-cigarette wholesale, retail side for many years now. So I know how confusing it can be for a newcomer. In this book, My goal is to break down all the changes by generation and show you how this industry has evolved for the better and how you can now finally quit the nasty habit of smoking real cigarettes and have a smooth transition into the new age of cleaner and much healthier alternative- e-cigarettes.

When I got started with e-cigarettes after smoking regular cigarettes for almost three decades, the devices were sub-standard where they didn't produce enough vapor to satisfy my craving, nor the battery lasted long enough. So I was always walking around with 3-4 of those devices in my pocket so I can satisfy my craving for a whole work day. But they have come a long way since those days. Now you can buy just one device and carry an e-liquid bottle, and the batteries can last you a full day and a half before you have to recharge them.

The e-liquid industry has come a long way too, they are better in quality, in taste and now has fewer Carcinogens as most of them are now made in the U.S. Stay away from Chinese made e -liquid if you can, they are by far the cheapest but not good in quality.

For any updates or where to buy and what to buy you can always check my blog at:
http://BestElectronicCigaretteHQ.com

Enjoy and Happy Vaping!

2. New Safety and Regulation

There have been a lot of changes in this industry as far as regulations are concerned; I would like to share what has been happening as far the regulations are concern so you are up-to-date on it.

Since the beginning, the Food and Drug Administration (FDA) has been greatly involved in the regulation of electronic cigarettes. As more and more research is completed and studies are conducted, the FDA may get closer to approval. The electronic cigarette market is still relatively new. This means a lot of governments are still trying to determine the right legislation to get a handle on this new and changing market. It wasn't until recently that the FDA started to make a focused effort on regulating the production and sale of electronic cigarettes and their associated parts. Let's first take a look at the history of the FDA and electronic cigarettes to understand the most recent developments.

While there are many events with electronic cigarettes that relate to FDA events, it all really started in 2006 when electronic cigarettes were first introduced in the United States. Of course, the FDA was alerted immediately due to the affiliation between electronic cigarettes and traditional tobacco cigarettes; this is also the reason why the FDA raised concerns about health.

In 2009, the FDA banned the U.S. Customs and Border Protection from allowing any electronic cigarettes of any kind to enter into the country. In May of 2009, the Action on Smoking and Health (ASH) filed a petition for the FDA to regulate electronic cigarettes. This was when the FDA started testing two specific brands of electronic cigarettes: NJOY and Smoking Everywhere. The results of this test showed findings of trace amounts of a group of carcinogens that is found in tobacco. Also, some cartridges that were labeled as 0mg of nicotine still contained small amounts of nicotine. In June, President Obama signed a law to give the FDA the ability to regulate tobacco products by passing the Family Smoking Prevention and Tobacco Control Act 18.

In April of 2011, the FDA started to regulate electronic cigarettes the same way it regulated other tobacco products through the Food, Drug, and Cosmetics Act. Labels on electronic cigarette products that discussed anything related to the product assisting with quitting smoking or having health benefits were strictly regulated as a device of a drug or medical purpose. Then in August of 2012, the FDA released a report of 100 people who had reported adverse health events from using electronic cigarettes.

In September 2013, the American Academy of Pediatrics (AAP) got involved. They urged the FDA to regulate tobacco products including cigars, cigarettes, and electronic cigarettes. In April 2014, the FDA required that electronic cigarettes would go under review where they could be approved for banning sales to minors and requiring warning labels on products. The AAP stated that electronic cigarettes were poisonous to children, which lead the FDA to propose a regulation on electronic cigarettes and gain control over tobacco products. In June 2014, the White House modified the ruling of the FDA on tobacco regulations and allowed electronic cigarettes to be sold online. However, in August, the FDA was urged by the American Heart Association (AHA) to conduct more research on electronic cigarettes as if they were tobacco and nicotine products so there could be more regulations on sales and marketing to youth. In September, the FDA proposed regulations on the sale of electronic cigarettes and other tobacco products to anyone under the age of 18 and all labels needed to include a list of ingredients. This is also the time when cigarette smokers were starting to choose electronic cigarettes as a means to quit smoking as more discussion was circulating about electronic cigarettes being a healthier option.

As the electronic cigarette market progressed and became more popular among traditional smokers and non-smokers alike, the FDA was urged by many to start regulating electronic cigarette products and their related parts. In May of 2016, the ruling was finalized that the FDA could extend its authority from just tobacco products to include electronic cigarettes and their parts under the Family Smoking Prevention and Tobacco Control Act of 2009.

Until 2016 there was no federal law prohibiting the sale of electronic cigarettes, e-hookah, vape juice or e-cigars to people under the age of 18. The FDAs new regulations are primarily designed to keep high school aged children from picking up an unnecessary nicotine habit and to prevent those who aren't currently smoking to start the habit.

As of May 2016, the FDA stated that they would be in control of regulating electronic cigarettes and their associated parts. Parts don't include accessories; but does include mouthpieces, tanks, atomizers, e-liquids, flavorings, e-juice containers, and batteries. All products going to market need to be FDA approved before they can be sold. This is a huge step forward for FDA electronic cigarette regulations and one of the biggest and most controlling steps. Many have issues with these new regulations, claiming that they will negatively impact the vaporizer and electronic cigarette market in the United States.

These new regulations also include packaging details, such as necessary health labels on every product package. E-juice retailers are no longer allowed to provide free samples and as with cigarette sales, a photo ID is required in order to make a purchase.

While many electronic cigarette smokers have said that they are safer than traditional cigarettes; until 2016 there was no guarantee about the products and ingredients going into cartridges or vape juice. Along with new FDA regulations, there was still the fact that the FDA doesn't have a definitive say as to what goes into vape juice. This would finally bring some order to the chaos of e-juice manufacturing and distribution in America since 2006.

Until 2016, there was very little regulation on the vaporizer and electronic cigarette market from the FDA. After many studies, it was decided that there should be stricter regulations on the growing electronic cigarette market. These regulations started in May 2016, but won't be fully in effect until 2017 or 2018.

WHAT THE FDA RULES WILL DO

The FDA is now able to regulate all tobacco products including electronic cigarettes, cigars, hookah tobacco and pipe tobacco. Prior to these changes the FDA only had oversight of cigarettes, cigarette tobacco, roll-your-own tobacco, and smokeless tobacco products.

The new regulation bans the sale of all types of tobacco products to people under the age of 18, requires a photo ID from buyers younger than 26, prohibits that sale of such products from vending machines (except in adult-only facilities) and prohibits the distribution of free samples.

Lastly, the regulation requires all products to carry warnings that they contain nicotine which is an addictive chemical. Nearly all electronic cigarettes and any new tobacco products now need to seek marketing authorization from the FDA. Any product sold before February 15, 2007, is exempt.

When Do the New Rules Take Effect?

The new rules are going to take effect in stages. The ban on sales to minors starts first on August 8th and will primarily affect Michigan and Pennsylvania. Currently, the other 48 states already ban the sales of electronic cigarettes to people under the age of 18. Coincidentally, California Governor Jerry Brown signed legislation that raised the legal smoking age in California from 18 to 21, prohibited the use of electronic cigarettes in many public places and banned the marketing of electronic cigarettes to children. These laws were to take effect on June 9th, making California the second state to raise the legal smoking age to 21 after Hawaii.

The prohibitions on giving out free samples and distribution from vending machines will also begin on August 8th. Retailers will also be required to ask buyers for photo identification. The warning label requirements don't go into effect until May 2018. Products already available on the market could remain for at least three more years. This is because manufacturers have two years to submit product applications to the FDA for review and the FDA has an additional year in order to finish their evaluation.

WHY ALL THE CHANGES?

While cigarette smoking has declined in the past few decades among both youths and adults; the use of other tobacco products, including electronic cigarettes, continues to increase. The FDA conducted a survey along with the Centers for Disease Control and Prevention which showed that in 2014, 1 in 4 high school students and 1 in 13 middle school students reported using tobacco; meaning they had consumed one or more tobacco products within the previous 30 days. That means 4.6 million youths. The survey also showed the electronic cigarette use among high school students increased from 1.5 percent in 2011 to 13.4 percent in 2014. Meanwhile, hookah use dramatically increased from 4.1 percent to 7.2 percent.

The focus of the new FDA regulations on electronic cigarettes is to make them more difficult for minors to access while also requiring some products to undergo rigorous, expensive scientific review. All the regulations were are part of the 2009 Tobacco Control Act passed by Congress. In May, the FDA announced that it would extend its authority to also include hookahs and premium cigars.

Buyers to tobacco and nicotine products who look younger than 27 must now show their ID to make a purchase, and undercover agents will go into stores to make sure that no minors are being allowed to purchase them. Additionally, the FDA will have authority to approve tobacco products no previously regulated that have gone on sale after February 15, 2007. During the new two years, companies will need to apply to have their products undergo rigorous and costly scientific review by the FDA. Electronic cigarette companies can only continue to sell their products for a year after application as they wait for the process to be completed.

The reason for these changes has to do with how electronic cigarettes work. The battery-powered devices heat a liquid nicotine solution that turns into a vapor users can inhale. Public health officials are worried that some of the flavors, such as bubble gum, will appeal to teens and children. Data from the Centers for Disease Control and Prevention also show that while teen cigarette smoking has decreased, the use and experimentation of electronic cigarettes have increased 900 percent.

According to the CDC, electronic cigarettes are considered unsafe because they contain nicotine. However, the debate continues over how electronic cigarettes compare with traditional cigarettes when it comes to the effects on a person's health. The FDA has said it needs more evidence in order to make a determination.

Without the new FDA regulation, customers wouldn't have a guarantee that the product they are used was made in sanitary conditions and that the listed ingredients; including the nicotine levels, are accurate.

While banning the sales of electronic cigarettes to minors isn't controversial since most states already have such laws, vaping proponents are fearful that the new regulatory requirements will drive the industry underground and that the review will likely cause a ban. Their argument is that many people who switch to electronic cigarettes use them as a pathway to eventually quit smoking altogether.

Gregory Conley, the president of the American Vaping Association, stated in an email: "Thanks to the FDA, it will now be easier for a new Marlboro cigarette to come to market than to continue marketing products believed by many health organizations to be at least 95 percent less hazardous than smoking."

While Congress has made efforts to move the date of enforcement back, these have not proceeded. Other portions of the Tobacco Control Act are ongoing; including the evaluation of effects of menthol cigarettes and creating graphic warning images to appear on cigarette packs. The

FDA has announced that their next focus is on proposing a rule to ban flavored cigars and another to make packaging more difficult for children to open.

3. PAST THREE GENERATIONS OF E–CIG

FIRST GENERATION OF ELECTRONIC CIGARETTE

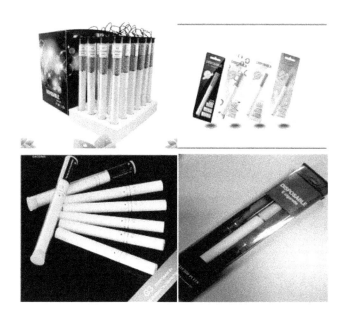

The first generation of electronic cigarettes is also sometimes referred to as Cig-a-Likes. This first generation of electronic cigarettes are roughly the same size as regular tobacco cigarettes and usually feature a similar look to traditional cigarettes, hence the term Cig-a-Likes. However, a Cig-a-Like is a big heavier than a traditional cigarette and has a LED light on the end of the device that lights up when inhaling.

The majority of the people who aren't familiar with electronic cigarettes immediately think of these types. This is because this type of electronic cigarette is easily accessible, cheap and easy to use; also they are often used in the media to portray anything linked with electronic cigarettes or vaping.

There are a few types of Cig-a-Likes that are disposable, meaning that you can vape on them until the non-reusable battery discharges and after that, you simply throw them away. However, there are some Cig-a-Likes that have rechargeable batteries and replaceable cartridges known as cartomizers.

These electronic cigarettes are often the first choice for newcomers because these models look and feel similar to traditional cigarettes. It is also a good way to try out electronic cigarettes at a minimal cost.

Most Cig-a-Likes are auto models, meaning they work automatically without an on/off function. On inhale, the suction will operate a switch that turns on the atomizer heater oil. There are a few models that are manual and have a small button near the top end of the battery. Each type has their own pros and cons to consider.

While there are hundreds of brand names to choose from with these electronic cigarettes, they are based on a few model types with a recognized series number that distinguishes them from others by their thread type and fit. In other words, a Whizzocig will turn out to be a KR808. If you know the model series then you can interchange the parts from other vendors since they will almost certainly fit. There are no proprietary models despite what manufacturers may claim; all electronic cigarettes belong to a specific series type. For example, the V2Cig and V4L are both KR808 models.

These models are referred to as first generation models because they were the first to be invented. Originally, all of these models had a three-piece system: a battery, an atomizer, and a cartridge. Now, most of these models use a two-piece system: a battery and a cartomizer. The cartomizer combines the atomizer and the liquid reservoir into one unit.

Polls show that people still continue to use these models frequently. Although not many continue to use these as their primary electronic cigarette, but they do use them as a back-up, loan or travel model. The batteries range from 125mAh size up to about 280mAh.

These electronic cigarettes are good choices for when you want to be discreet or unobtrusive and have something with a low profile. They can also be a good initiation into the electronic cigarette market. Even though these can be used anywhere you would smoke a cigarette; it still isn't a good idea to try using it indoors because people will still assume you are smoking. Although if you don't want to get it confused with a traditional cigarette, then you can consider getting a black one or one with a blue or green LED tip so that it looks less like a traditional cigarette.

Since battery size is everything in the electronic cigarette world, these first generation cigarettes don't have a great performance rating, and there isn't much that can be done to remedy this situation. For example, a 20-a-day former smoker would need at least six batteries in order to get continuous use, and that's a lot of batteries to have to keep with you. These first generation cigarettes are best for two different uses: introducing new users to the concept of vaping and use by the occasional smoker. The most common first generation models include: Ego, 510, 901, M401 and KR808. Lately in the last 3 generation, mostly what you see is ego style or 510 style threads. One thing to remember if you have a battery that takes Ego style atomizers, chances are it will also take a 510 atomizers, but on the other hand a 510 type battery will not take an Ego style atomizers. Take a look at both types of batteries in the picture.

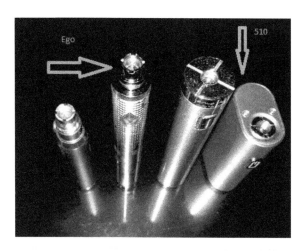

The most important thing about these first generation electronic cigarettes is that they look like traditional tobacco cigarettes, which means new users are typically happier to try them compared to the newer larger models even though they are more efficient. However, these models don't deliver enough nicotine to the user. Multiple clinical trials have shown that for many these devices act mostly as a placebo. Blood plasma nicotine level tests reveal that little or no nicotine is delivered. This is a product of low performance, poor vaping technique by new users and too low a nicotine strength for the combination of low performance and poor technique. There are two solutions to help with this. First, you can use much higher nicotine strength if you have a craving. For example, 45mg (4.5%) strength is shown to be required in some cases, depending on the device efficiency. Second, you can upgrade to a more efficient device, which will be a larger device. Alternately, you can learn better user technique, which may solve the problem in some cases.

So let's take a look at the specific advantages and disadvantages to these first generation electronic cigarettes:

Advantages:

- Looks and feels like a traditional cigarette.

- Small and discreet.

- Auto and manual models.

- The cheapest way to get started with electronic cigarettes.

- Parts can be re-used if you know the model type.

- Ideal for light smokers or occasional smokers.

Disadvantages:

- Batteries don't last long in use - from 45 minutes to 2 hours for some users.

- Other generations of electronic cigarettes have better performance.

- Will probably not provide sufficient performance for heavy smokers or full-flavor smokers.

- The auto batteries can be destroyed by liquid leaking down into the battery due to over-enthusiastic refilling.

- Cannot use LR heads - the minimum resistance these small devices can run is about 2ohms which limits vapor production.

The last thing to discuss with first generation electronic cigarettes is backups. Those who are new to vaping won't quite appreciate the need for backups when it comes to every item: battery, head, refills, and charger. Any item can fail at any time, and this will leave you in a difficult position. All the parts of an electronic cigarette system are consumable; there is no such thing as an electronic cigarette for life, and most items require replacement. Two items that newcomers typically under purchase at first are batteries and refills.

When it comes to batteries, the minimum practical number to have on hand is three: one in use, one charging, and one

extra "on hand". Users of these first generation electronic cigarettes will often need more than this since the battery typically only lasts an hour before needing to be recharged. The smaller the battery, the more you are going to need.

The atomizer or head will also need a spare. These can be cartomizers, clearomizers, tanks or RBAs (re-buildable). Some models have a replaceable atomizer wick cartridge. A basic atomizer such as a 510 with a drip tip is very useful for testing new flavors.

You should always have plenty of refill liquid on hand. If you buy your e-liquid on the internet, you will also need to have extra in reserve to account for delivery times that can be extended, so you aren't left without any supplies.

Lastly, there is the charger. Don't forget to have at least one of these in reserve. A battery charger can fail and then you won't have any way to charge your vaporizer.

Experience electronic cigarette users know you need to have backups for your backups. While this may seem like a high initial cost, the reality is it costs far less than traditional smoking, especially in places where taxes are substantial.

The second generation of electronic cigarettes looks more like a pen or laser pointer and are substantially larger than first generation electronic cigarettes. When using a second generation electronic cigarette, you need to manually press the fire button while inhaling. The batteries for these personal vaporizers have a much larger capacity; about three to seven times larger than the previous generation or 450-1100mAh. This means that in most cases, you can have vaping power for a day or two.

The battery for a second generation electronic cigarette typically features a 510 threaded connection which provides quite a wide compatibility with atomizers/clearomizers. A few of these second generation models will also allow you to adjust the voltage either with the help of two tiny buttons or by twisting the base of the battery. The most popular batteries for second generation electronic cigarettes are the eGo style batteries. These are typically paired with entry-level clearomizers like Innokin iClear 16, Aspire ET-s or a Kanger E-vod.

The second generation or mid-size electronic cigarette is the top rated model because it suits most vapers whether they are using it as a main device or just a main back-up. The most common names for this generation include eGo, Riva, Tornado and kGo.

The benchmark model is the mid-size electronic cigarette with a clearomizer. These are about the size of a slim cigar. Nearly all models of the second generation electronic cigarettes are manual; very few auto batteries are made. Some models allow you to select the voltages around 3 or 4 steps from 3.3 volts to 4.5 volts or so.

Since these second generation electronic cigarettes have a much larger battery size, there are three important results. First, the batteries will last longer when in use. Second, they will produce more vapor than first generation models. Third, you can use a wider range of heads. You can use all kinds of tanks and other exotic heads. Perhaps the most important factor is that they can use the LR or low resistance type of atomizer coil in the head, which allows you to produce more vapors.

Perhaps the biggest advantage to this model is that it is considered the basic electronic cigarette, so it has a wide range of accessories to choose from. However, a big disadvantage to consider is the fact that the eGo type has experienced more battery fires that all other types of electronic cigarettes put together. Most of the fires have occurred when the unit is being charged. This can either be from overall low quality or the wrong charger being used. This is due to the fact that there is a wide availability of cheap clones and ultra-cheap chargers on the market. If you use original and genuine models, then you are unlikely to suffer any mishaps.

Clones of this model are sometimes made too cheaply. This cheapness means low quality, which equals fire while being charged. To avoid this risk, there are three things you can do. First, charge all mid-sized units in a Li-Po charging sack which is a special fireproof bag for unstable batteries. Second, never recharge your electronic cigarette in a room where oxygen is in use or available. Third, carefully monitor the elderly or confused person when using an electronic cigarette.

Let's recap the main advantages and disadvantages to second generation electronic cigarettes:

Advantages:

- Can use LR accessories, down to about 1.5ohms.

- They aren't too expensive to get started, maybe 50% more than a first generation electronic cigarette; but you must pay more in order to get good quality so always buy a good brand and not a clone if you are in doubt.

- The 510 connector type most commonly used has a wide range of heads.

- The smallest battery choice, the 650mAh, is reasonably small for those who want a discreet electronic cigarette. While you can use a 450mAh battery for these units, it won't have much of a charge time in use.

- It looks and feels like a small cigar so it's not overly big.

- It doubles the performance of a first generation electronic cigarette in both vapor and battery life.

- The batteries last well when in use; the bigger batteries of 1,000mAh can last up to eight hours for some vapers.

- Provide sufficient performance for most smokers switching to electronic cigarettes, especially newcomers.

- Rated the top electronic cigarette since it suits more users than any other type.

Disadvantages:

- They are nearly exclusively manual electronic cigarettes. Although this is only a disadvantage of newcomers, but can actually be an advantage to experienced users.

- May seem too large for beginners.

- Slightly more expensive starting costs.

- Ultimate performance isn't possible due to the battery power/voltage still not being sufficient.

- You need to be aware of cheap clones and/or cheap chargers that can cause fires.

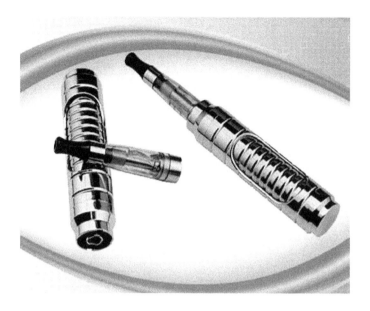

It is often hard to identify these electronic cigarettes simply by their looks. The fact is these Advanced Personal Vaporizers (APVs) come in many different shapes and sizes. They can range from the shape of a screwdriver to a box the size of a big, bulky smart phone. However, in most cases, they are considerably larger than first generation Cig-a-Likes or second generation electronic cigarettes. Nearly all third generation models feature a manual fire button, so they are considered a manual electronic cigarette.

The main element of third generation electronic cigarettes is a 'mod' or the power source. There are two types of mods for this generation of electronic cigarette.

First are the mechanical mods. This is actually a very simple device since it has no electronic circuitry. These mods feature only a fire button, a battery compartment (usually for an 18650 type) and a connector. However, they aren't suitable for every vaper. While they are simple, some knowledge and the ability to put things together when it comes to volts, watts, ohms and amps is required in order to safely use them. Although for advanced users, mechanical mods have become favorites because, when used properly, these devices can be very effective in delivering plenty of flavorful vapors.

Second are the regulated mods. These are more complex than the mechanical mods since they incorporate control hardware that lets the vaper modify the voltage and/or wattage output while often having additional features like electrical resistance meters, as well as safety features like reverse battery polarity protection. Regulated mods can be very powerful, but they are also more user-friendly than the mechanical mods.

Whether the mods are mechanical or regulated, they are usually paired with different kinds of atomizers: either a standard clearomizer, a sub-ohm thank, a re-buildable atomizer or a re-buildable tank atomizer.

APVs are a logical progression and development on the electronic cigarette concept for those seeking the ultimate performance. They are simply defined as any model that employs user-replaceable generic batteries and/or has a function not normally available in a mini or mid-sized electronic cigarette. So an APV can simply be a battery holder tube, or it can be the Ferrari of the electronic cigarette world that has all the bells and whistles.

There are two main classes of APV: tubular shaped tubemods and box shaped boxmods. So this basically means they normally look like a fat tube like a flashlight with a mouthpiece or a box the size of a pack of cigarettes with a mouthpiece.

These types of electronic cigarettes don't typically suit newcomers since they are too big and weird looking or too difficult to use. In addition to the fact that they are all manual-switch models. Almost all of them have a huge extended battery life over first generation models and they typically use generic 3.7 volt lithium ion cells, a type of rechargeable battery that can be bought from a variety of sources. There are several types of batteries, but the most popular one is the 18650 IMR (Li-ion) rechargeable battery. See picture below.

The biggest advantage is the performance of these third generation models that comes with the large batteries. In addition, the advanced functions and features that are available according to the various individual models make them appealing: integral liquid feed, digital readout, variable voltage, full electronic control, solid metal construction or attractive wooden construction with inlays and so on.

It is best that a newcomer doesn't purchase an APV, but rather a first or second generation electronic cigarette so that it is easier to gain familiarity with all the many aspects of vaping. This will also give the newcomer a better appreciation of the many issues when choosing an APV later on after gaining experience. There is a wide variety of choices that can be confusing at first and getting started with cheaper models first is best.

Let's consider a breakdown of the most important advantages and disadvantages of the third generation electronic cigarette.

Advantages:

- Great performance gains: three times or more than the first generation. Offering three to ten times more vapor volume than small electronic cigarettes.

- Extended battery life.

- Solid construction.

- Some of the base units have the potential to last a lifetime.

- The advanced functions are very useful to an experienced user.

- Digital micro-electronics help with power control, readouts and so on.

- Simple and rugged mechanical units are available that are highly reliable.

- Batteries last a very long time in use; the average is about eight hours although some can last for days.

- Provides sufficient performance for any traditional smoker.

Disadvantages:

- Expensive to get started with some base units costing over $200, though there are some cheaper models.

- They are only available as manual models. Again a disadvantage to newcomers, but an advantage to experienced users.

- Some care with battery charging is advised since you need to treat large lithium ion cells with respect.

- Some vapers can eventually migrate to 'extreme vaping' with APVs, such as sub-ohming and cloud-chasing. This means the risk reduction isn't as generous with this type of use.

- Extreme vaping along with mechanical mods and poor battery choice has resulted in explosive events. These risks are significantly elevated with the use of counterfeit batteries.

While these are the three main generations of electronic cigarettes leading up to the newest generation, it is worthwhile to take the time to mention some notable sub-types as well as historic models.

MICRO

Originally, there were also many micro or 'super-mini' models. These were slightly shorter than the first generation Cig-a-Likes. While a regular 510 can also have short batteries, it isn't technically correct to say that the micros were always smaller, but it was the general situation. These models suited people who were perhaps reluctant in the early days. Today, these models aren't popular since the batteries only last a few minutes, and the performance is now vastly better.

PEN STYLE

These models were very popular for several years since they filled the gap between the first generation and the third generation electronic cigarettes. This was before the gap was filled successfully by the mid-size second generation models such as the eGo. These models received their name because they were almost exactly the same size as a fountain pen and some even looked like one, with a characteristic step in the level of the tube near one end that made it look as if it had a pen cap.

Pen styles tended to be more auto than manual. The most popular feature of these models was the 801 thread system that was common among them, such as the DSE801. This was the best thread system ever used on an electronic cigarette since it is slightly larger, stronger, more reliable and generally more robust. The pen styles also used larger atomizers and cartridges than other modes like the 510 and KR808. However, these older three-piece systems were notorious for leaking, and this is one of the main reasons why the market shifted to the two piece cartomizer system. No one made cartos for the 801 thread and the second generation eventually replaced the pen style. While these are still found on the market they are primarily a niche product now and no used much in the United States, but the most often seen model is the Ruyan V8.

XL Mini

As the pen styles died out, some first generation models started coming with an XL option. This was mostly found in the KR808 series. These can be 143mm long and could be seen as a way to stay with the KR8 thread system and get a larger battery capacity without having to upgrade to the second generation model, which is often 510-based. The typical XL Mini model has a long, steel battery. Manual buttons are more often seen on these than any other type of mini model.

6 VOLT MODS

Before VV and even before the 5 volt regulated APVs, custom devices developed from plain metal tubes with generic lithium batteries. The first was the Screwdriver from the UK, followed my many others. These models used one 3.7 volt rechargeable cell. At the time the only head option was the SR atomizer (2.3 ohms) and it didn't produce a perfect vape with all refills; there were no LR heads, no RBAs, no clearos even. So in order to get a stronger vape you needed two cells stacked to create the 6 Volt Mod. If you do the math, you can see that these APVs actually get 8.4 volts at full charge. This burns out regular atomizers, so HR accessories were then required: 3.5 / 4 / 4/5 ohm versions were seen.

With these devices, there was a serious elevation of risk for a violent or even explosive battery failure since it was common to stack two unprotected Li-ion cells. In a sealed or semi-sealed metal tube, the consequences of doing this with unstable cells subject to uncontrollable thermal runaway especially when paired are obvious. Violent failures occurring in stacked unprotected RC123a Li-ion cells in metal tube devices produced legendary events which luckily were few in number but attracted plenty of attention.

Eventually, technology saved the day and 5 Volt regulated, then VV variable voltage devices, then VW and RBAs replaced the 6 Volt tube mods. VV / VW or RBA devices are now most commonly used, so technology has moved on. Enthusiasts still use mechanical mods, which have seen a revival due to the popularity of RBAs, but they are much safer now due to different batteries available rather than the dangerous unprotected Li-ion cells. A full power vape can now be obtained using a single cell, either with electronics VV or VW; or with an RBA atomizer. The growing popularity of 26650 cells in giant mechanical mods also allows for the most powerful vape and length of time between charges ever possible with electronic cigarettes.

FOURTH GENERATION ELECTRONIC CIGARETTE

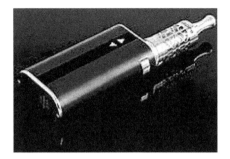

While most categorize electronic cigarettes into the three main generations already discussed, there is a fourth generation that should be added to the list. This is to help distinguish the most recent, most powerful, most advanced and most innovated device on the market.

This new generation features mods with automatic temperature control and the ability to handle very low ohm builds, as well as sub-ohm clearomizers (or rebuildable tanks) themselves featuring adjustable and dual airflow slots. All of these mods are far superior to the first and second generation electronic cigarettes, and they are much more advanced than the majority of the mods released in 2014.

MY TAKE

Now that I explained all four generations of e-cigarette devices let me also mention that if you are just starting out, don't go and buy the most expensive or most complicated device at first. Instead, buy a 2nd or 3rd generation device that has a good battery and a great atomizer. Try it first and see how you like and enjoy the experience. Just because some of these devices are from the previous generation, doesn't mean they are inferior in quality. As a matter of fact even today I still vape a 2nd generation Vamo (See the picture) with a high powered atomizer, and this device runs on 18650 battery which last two days at minimum. So again the point I am trying to make is, don't go buy a $200 mod or a kit when you can spend $50 and enjoy a great vaping experience. Once you become more familiar with this new world, then you can venture into more complicated gadgets and devices but at first stay with something simple yet powerful. (Here are two devices that I still use today)

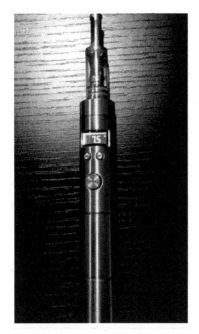

Last year I started importing some e-cigarette kits that are Bluetooth enable, meaning you can connect to the device via your phone or any other Bluetooth devices. Why do you need to do that? Well, some people want the Bluetooth option where they can adjust ohm (resistance), or the wattage (power) via their phone and not directly on the device. To me, that is overkill, though I sold a lot of those devices through my wholesale channel but I personally didn't like those at all.

4. Advantages of Fourth Generation Electronic Cigarettes

So just what makes these fourth generation models better than all the rest? Basically, innovation has led to a safe and more customizable vapor device than ever before. You can now get an electronic cigarette that you can adjust its setting in a number of ways in order to suit your individual needs. Consider the main advantage you get from this generation.

- Extremely long charge time.

- Small and compact size.

- Adjustable voltage/wattage.

- Adjustable air flow.

- Temperature sensing.

- Vastly superior to previous generations.

The Life Span of the 4th Generation Devices

One of the most common questions people ask when it comes to electronic cigarettes is how much do they cost. Along with this common question, something people will ask as well includes: How long should a battery last? How long does a cartomizer last? How long will a pack of electronic cigarettes get me? I will help answer these questions to make it clearer for those who are getting started with electronic cigarettes and what they can expect.

First, I need to start by stating that there is no single and clear answer to these questions. The exact longevity and cost of vapor smoking can vary greatly based on the individual vapor smoker's type of unit and style of smoking. Modern electronic cigarettes offer the freedom to choose from many difference smoking experiences, meaning each individual nicotine habit comes with its own unique cost levels and life span compared to another individual based on their nicotine habit.

How Long Should a Battery Last?

The biggest question first time electronic cigarette users have is when buying a starter kit, how often they will have to recharge their battery. While the majority of the battery life is going to depend on the frequency of use, there are a few standard figures that will help the new user to determine what type of battery they should order.

Most modern models of electronic cigarettes, including those made by Eversmoke, are powered by a standard capacity lithium-ion battery that can be used much longer than the disposable batteries of previous electronic cigarette generations and they also tend to have faster recharges when required. In a single cycle, one battery can last months; but eventually, it is going to wear out and need to be replaced entirely.

However, between charges the size of an electronic cigarette battery will determine how long it will power the unit. Eversmoke, the most common manufacturer, offers three choices depending on how frequently you vape:

- Mini - Lasts up to 175 puffs

- Standard - Lasts up to 250 puffs

- High-Capacity - Lasts up to 350 puffs

A typical battery is going to take up to 250 charges before needing to be replaced. So this means that with a high-capacity battery you are likely to get about 87,000 puffs before needing to get a replacement battery. If you are a high-frequency vaper you are going to need to recharge sooner or about every two hours; whereas a low-frequency vaper can expect a battery to last anywhere from four to eight hours.

It is typically recommended that new vapor smokers prepare themselves by having at least two batteries on hand. This way you can alternate between recharging a battery and vaping. For most average smokers, these two batteries are enough to power an electronic cigarette all day. It is always a good idea to look at your individual vaping style and determine exactly how many batteries to have on hand. And make sure you order more in time, so you don't need a replacement and have to wait.

Lastly, in addition to your vaping style, there are also seven things you can do to care for your battery that will increase the overall longevity of the battery.

5. How To Care for Your Devices

Use the Battery Regularly

This is similar to the reasoning behind exercising regularly. Your electronic cigarette batteries will benefit from regular use. The more a battery performs, the easier power will flow through the battery cells. The lithium-ion batteries used in electronic cigarettes are designed for daily use, which is why the same types of batteries are also commonly found in cell phones.

Be Careful Where you Store your Battery

While this typically seems like common sense, it is easy to get careless and not fully think about something that can harm the device. When it comes to electronic cigarette batteries, direct sunlight and heat can dramatically affect the lifespan. Everyone knows that electricity and water don't mix, so it is always good to keep batteries away from water. It is also good to be mindful of impacts so prevent your battery from being dropped or otherwise sustaining a bit hit.

Change your Battery Before It's Drained

Many experienced vapers have a rotation of batteries on hand for this reason. If you wait until the battery is fully drained before plugging it into a charger is certainly going to reduce the life of your battery. Rather, it is best to recharge the battery when you've used the available power and ideally when you start noticing a loss in power. A good illustration of this is a train. It is easier for a slow-moving train to speed up rather than a stationary train to start moving in the first place. Similarly, it is easier for a battery with some power left in it to be recharged than it is for a battery that is completely dead.

Don't Store a Battery with Less than 50% Charge

When you store a battery for future, use it should ideally have a full charge. If you store a battery that has a 50% or less charge, they will drain faster. Similar to the discussion in number three, the battery will have to work harder to deliver the power needed for the device. As with anything electrical, the harder it has to work the shorter its lifespan becomes.

Disconnect the Atomizer When Not in Use

You only really need to worry about this one when you aren't using your device for an extended period of time. The cartomizer is the part that contains the heating element and nicotine liquid, and it connects to the battery. Even when you aren't using your electronic cigarette, it is always draining a little bit of power. This is why disconnecting the cartomizer and battery can extend the time between charges, which will increase the number of recharges you can do and increase the time before you need to replace the battery entirely.

Unscrew the Battery When Finished Charging

After charging your battery take it off the charger as soon as possible. This will ensure you aren't overcharging the battery, which can overwork the device and reduce its lifespan. The only time you shouldn't do this is when you are charging the battery for the first time when you should leave it on the charger for an extra hour or so.

Keep Threads and Contacts on the Cartomizer and Battery Clean

The last thing you need to do to get a long battery life is to make sure you keep the contacts between the battery and the cartomizer clean. Over time, these contacts can get dirty and moist; which can ruin the battery. Use a cotton swab, Q-tip or alcohol pad and periodically wipe down the threads and contacts where the cartomizer and battery hook together.

All of these seven tips can work for both automatic and manual electronic cigarette batteries. However, there are a couple of tips that apply to each specific battery type.

AUTOMATIC BATTERY - Whenever you are finished vaping or otherwise using the device you should slightly unscrew the battery from the cartomizer. When these components are left tightly connected, it will drain the battery much quicker. It is definitely recommended to do this for any long-term storage of over a few hours, but it should always be done if you have an automatic battery.

MANUAL BATTERY - Avoid pressing the button on the battery too hard. When you do this, the button can stick or even fall into the battery.

6. How Long Should they Last?

The cartomizer is a combination of the cartridge and the atomizer. The atomizer typically needs to be replaced before the cartridge. There is a small metal coil in the atomizer that heats the e-juice, creating the nicotine-infused vapor that travels through the mouthpiece and into the lungs. These coils can get dry and burn out, requiring you to get a new cartomizer.

Cartomizers can last up to a year, but on average last only about a month or two. Again, much of this answer will depend on the type and frequency of use. As the cartomizer starts to fail, you will notice a change in the effectiveness of the unit's ability to vaporize the e-juice. Not only that, it will start to taste different or even give you a burnt taste, this means you will get a flavor that isn't as rich and thick as a properly functioning unit.

This is why it is essential to have an extra cartomizer on hand for all vapor smokers. Not only will this give you a backup in case a cartomizer fails, but it allows you also to alternate between uses so you are sure to notice when an electronic cigarette is losing its vapor production levels.

7. How Much Should you Expect to Spend in a Year?

Over the course of a year, the cost savings can really start to add up. The average cost of a pack of traditional cigarettes in the United States in around $6. If a smoker goes through a pack a day, the annual cost for a nicotine habit is $2,190; not including the cost of driving to the convenience store to get the cigarettes. In comparison, if a smoker switches to electronic cigarettes the estimated cost breakdown for an average user is something like 365 electronic cigarettes for $800 and two replacement high-capacity batteries for $46. Giving you a total annual cost of $846, saving you nearly 60% off traditional cigarettes. And this is just to start. Over the course of a few years, there are other benefits that save you additional money. Such as being able to order online to reduce travel costs. Also, there is less cost for medical treatment related to smoke exposure.

Consider exactly how you can save a lot of money with electronic cigarettes.

8. Ways Electronic Cigarettes Can Save you Money

For many smokers, the allure of electronic cigarettes is the money you will save, especially since the cost of traditional cigarettes is always on the rise. Then when you factor in the health concerns for cigarettes, it can seem pretty foolish to spend over $200 a month on a smoking habit that ultimately can lead to your death. So let's look at exactly how you can save money by switching to electronic cigarettes.

Short Run

In the beginning, an electronic cigarette starter kit may seem like an expensive thing to buy; but you need to consider the big picture. Consider how much you typically spend in a week on traditional cigarettes. While the amount isn't the same for every individual, the savings are going to be there no matter what.

A single cartridge is equal to about one pack of cigarettes and cartridges are about $3 a piece, which is dramatically lower than what most people spend on traditional cigarettes. In some cities, the cost of a pack of cigarettes can be as high as $11.

You also have to consider the fact that most electronic cigarette starter kits come with money back guarantees. This means you can return your products for a full refund if you decide that electronic cigarettes aren't for you. So even if you are skeptical about paying up front for a starter kit, you have the comfort of knowing you can return it if you choose. If you decide to keep it, the cost will become less noticeable over time because the savings of electronic cigarettes add up fast.

However, in the short term, you don't need a start kit. You can consider starting with just a single, disposable electronic cigarette. These cost about $10 apiece and are about the same as two traditional packs of cigarettes. Try one out and you can reduce your regular cigarette usage and thus reduce your short term costs.

LONG RUN

In the long run, the savings with electronic cigarettes become much more considerable. From a weekly cost to a monthly cost you will start feeling the savings immediately. If you look at the yearly cost for a pack a day habit and compare it to a cartridge a day, the savings are monumental. The only difference is with electronic cigarettes you need to purchase in advance, so you don't run out of cartridges at the wrong time. But by doing this, you aren't constantly spending money on cigarettes, which is a benefit for some.

OTHER WAYS YOU SAVE MONEY

When people switch off electronic cigarettes, they often notice they smoke less. They often aren't committed to smoking an entire cigarette whenever they want just a few puffs, which can increase the longevity of your cartridges without any discomfort. This is a nice side effect to electronic cigarettes, which allows individuals to lessen their usage and also their spending without losing the nicotine sensation.

Electronic cigarettes are also healthier which is an indirect way they save you money. Tobacco is unhealthy and has been proven to cause major health issues, which eventually cost a lot. Doctor and hospital visits, as well as medications definitely, come with a high price and the time to heal can also cost you lost wages at work. When you are healthier, your performance is also better as well. While it isn't guaranteed you won't get sick, not smoking tobacco is often considered a preventative measure against the common cold and flu by many health professionals.

Lastly, when you have electronic cigarettes, you won't have to cover up your habit. This will save you money in the cost of cologne or perfume in order to get rid of the smell of smoke. You also won't have to worry about the cost of small things like gum, lighters and ashtrays. While these may seem like small costs, they do add up over time.

Ultimately, the cost savings and the longevity of the electronic cigarette is going to depend on the individual user. However, many are learning that the benefits of electronic cigarettes are far superior to traditional smoking.

9. Easy Caring and Storage

Another way that you can extend the life of your electronic cigarette is by learning how to properly take care of it. One thing that should be at the top of your list is properly cleaning your device. As with anything, hygiene is always important. People would freak out if they know exactly how dirty the items they use on a daily basis really are and electronic cigarettes are no exception.

Probably the first and most common piece of advice is to not keep your electronic cigarette in a drawer or just lying around somewhere that allows everything to get on it. Rather always keep them in their protective case or holder. There are a number of accessories to choose from when it comes to the hygiene, convenience, and protection of your electronic cigarettes.

Cleaning Steps

In addition to storing in a protective carrying case, there are a few steps you can take to properly care for your vaping device. It isn't really that difficult of a process and doesn't require a lot of time or effort.

First, you need to have a sanitary, non-cluttered area when cleaning your electronic cigarette. You can put down several paper towels to help and have a few on hand.

Second, unscrew the atomizer to disassemble your electronic cigarette. If there is a drip protector on it, you should remove it as well.

Third, start with cleaning the atomizer. If you have started noticing a bad taste, it is likely because the atomizer needs to be cleaned. You shouldn't have to worry about this if you clean your atomizer regularly. Start with gently wiping the battery end of the atomizer to remove any leftover e-juice. Put the battery end to your lips and blow lightly to get out any of the liquid. Blow two to three times to make sure you have cleared it all out then take a paper towel and wipe it down gently again.

Next, clean the battery terminal by dipping a cotton swab in rubbing alcohol and gently scrubbing the connections of the battery. If you see a lot of gunk that is stuck on tight, then you can carefully scrape it off with a toothpick. Once all of the gunk is removed, use a cotton ball to rub the device. Allow the battery to completely dry before reassembling the device.

Clean the Inside and the Outer Thread

Lastly, put the electronic cigarette back together with a fully charged battery. Make sure everything is completely dry and carefully inspect for any leftover gunk. After putting it back together, wipe the outside down thoroughly to make sure all unwanted bacteria is removed. Then you only have to put it back in its case until the next use.

This entire process from start to finish should usually only take five to ten minutes. Not bad for something that can help increase the life of your electronic cigarette. Proper cleaning should always be at the top of the lift for all vapers when it comes to increasing the longevity of your device. It can also go a long way to enhancing the vaping experience.

PROPER STORAGE OF SUPPLIES

Even if you are new to vaping, you will likely amass a pile of electronic cigarette supplies pretty quickly. These supplies can include multiple automatic and manual batteries, bottles of different e-juice flavors, full and blank cartomizers and any number of vaping accessories. Experienced vapers can tell you that finding a place to store all of this can be a challenge in both organization and proper storage. Fortunately, there are a few simple solutions you can do to help properly store your electronic cigarette supplies.

LONG TERM STORAGE

When it comes to storing and organizing all of the bulking vaping supplies, any typical storage container or box will do. The most popular storage box for long-term use is a crafter's or fisherman's tackle box. The dividers and adjustable compartments in these boxes help to keep batteries, cartomizers, e-juice and accessories separate and organized. However, you can also use a simple Tupperware container to store all of your supplies in one place, but it just won't have the organization capacity of something like a tackle box.

If you purchase bulk supplies in advance for your electronic cigarette such as backup batteries, blank cartomizers or bottles of e-juice; then the most important thing to remember is to store them in a place where they won't be exposed to light, heat or moisture. All of these elements can shorten the performance and lifespan of an electronic cigarette and its components. It is best to store your bulk supplies in a cool, dark and dry place. Many experienced vapers find it best to store in a kitchen or bathroom cabinet or closet. When it comes to batteries, you should also avoid storing them in metal boxes that conduct electricity. This can shorten the battery and diminish its life span.

SHORT TERM STORAGE

Experienced vapers will tell you that it is recommended to have at least one extra battery and cartomizer handy as a backup at all times. This way you can ensure your vapor smoking experience isn't interrupted by a dead battery or an empty cartomizer. However, this also means that there is usually an extra electronic cigarette or two lying around ready to be used or having to be carried with you when you go somewhere.

The biggest question a new user will have is whether or not to store these daily use vaping supplies. There are a number of specially designed electronic cigarette stands and containers that you can buy at the store in order to hold your supplies throughout the day. However, experienced vapers have come up with a clever and resourceful idea by using a toothbrush holder. If you are using a slim electronic cigarette model, then the battery and cartomizer will slide right not the toothbrush slot so you can easily grab them as you head out the door. There is also the simpler option of storing them in a glass or coffee mug. Anything portable that keeps your cartomizers standing up so that the e-juice doesn't leak into the cartridge is going to work for short-term storage. Just make sure you don't put it in the wrong cup and submerge your electronic cigarette in liquid.

Travel Storage

Electronic cigarettes are the perfect choice for frequent travelers. Not only do they provide you the freedom to vape when and where ever you want, but most of the supplies are compact, light and easily transportable. If you are on a trip and need a safe way to transport all of your electronic cigarette supplies then there are several options available to you depending on the amount of supplies you will need to bring and how long you plan to travel.

For example, if you are going to be on an extended trip you can consider a pencil pouch which is found in the school supplies section of any local store. Or if you need more room you can consider a toiletry bag. For shorter trips, you may be able to simply use a makeup bag or coin pouch in order to store your supplies.

SPECIALTY STORAGE

While tackle boxes are certainly the best option for storing bulk vaping supplies, where should you store your everyday electronic cigarette? There are a number of accessories on the market to make vapor smoking stylish and convenient. There is no shortage of universal carrying cases made from metal to protect them from crushing. These carrying cases often have room for your electronic cigarette, two refill cartridges, and a USB charger; all while fitting comfortably in your pocket.

Another convenient option is the lanyard. These allow you to keep your favorite electronic cigarette right around your neck, where it is ready to be used whenever you need it. This is perfect for those who want functionality and minimalism.

These are just a few of the most common ideas for storing and organizing your collection of vaping supplies. As you can experience, you can try out various storage ideas and find one that works best for your individual needs.

10. Proper Care and Maintenance for Maximum Lifespan

When you take proper care and maintenance of your electronic cigarette, then you can save both time and money by extending the longevity of your vapor smoking device. However, this doesn't mean you need to take hours caring for your electronic cigarette. In fact, most electronic cigarettes have the excellent benefit of being relatively maintenance free. Basically, all you have to do to prepare a device for the day's use is to screw in a new pre-filled cartridge and occasionally recharge the battery. That's all there is to it.

However, as with any piece of electronic equipment, sometimes an electronic cigarette will need a little extra care in order to operate at its full potential for the lifetime of the device. For example, some smokers notice that after time their vapor isn't as thick or strong as it was at the start or some may notice that the battery is starting to malfunction. Thankfully, it is pretty easy to get your electronic cigarette back to peak performance with a few quick and easy cleaning and maintenance steps.

Cartridges, Atomizers and Cartomizers

Most of the electronic cigarette models on the market today are a two-piece technology consisting of the cartridge and the battery. The cartridge is also known as the cartomizer. This also has two components - a built-in atomizer and the cartridge that holds the e-liquid and delivers it to the user as they inhale through the silicone mouthpiece. At one time, atomizers and cartridges were sold as two separate parts, but there was a lot of hassle with keeping a three-piece system clean, so most models have now combined these components. This has virtually eliminated the need for any maintenance with this end of the electronic cigarette.

Some manufacturers even go a step further by making vapor smokers that have pre-filled cartridges. This means you don't have to figure out how to properly refill e-liquid or worry about cleaning up afterward. The cartridges are designed and prepared to ensure you get a clean, smooth draw and the maximum vapor with each breath. After using up a cartridge, you simply discard it and get a new pre-filled cartridge with no cleaning needed.

Tips to Make your Cartridge Last Longer

As with most things you own, taking care of things is a top priority in order to save both time and money. When a traditional cigarette smoker takes two puffs of a cigarette and throws it away, they are wasting a lot of money. Although the same can also be said for those, who are using an electronic cigarette. In order to get the most money out of your vaping experience, you need to follow some basic tips to help make your electronic cigarette cartridge last as long as possible.

The cartridge is the part of your device that contains your electronic cigarette's flavored nicotine liquid. The cartridge is an important component for storing the nicotine and liquid flavor that creates the vaping pleasure. The nicotine solution, which can be both nicotine and non-nicotine based, is diluted with propylene glycol (PG). The solution is heated and vaporized by the atomizer before being transported to the mouthpiece.

Consider the following tips to help you extend the life of your cartridge:

● If you aren't using your cartridge for an extended period of time, then you should remove it from the electronic cigarette battery.

● After removing the cartridge, store it in a cool place. Never leave the cartridge in a hot or rainy environment. Also, don't place it in the freezer.

● When you are ready to use the cartridge again, make sure it has the time needed to adjust to room temperature before vaping in order to ensure it works properly.

- Don't blow in a cartridge since it can actually damage the cartridge or flood the battery with liquid and damage the battery.

- Every now and then you should switch out the cartridge even if it still has some life to it. It gives the current cartridge a rest from the heat and allows the liquid to disperse. It will also give you a chance to change flavors.

- If your electronic cigarette is starting to act sluggish or isn't achieving maximum output, then you shouldn't automatically think something is wrong with the cartridge. It may be that the battery needs to be charged, or there can be another issue. Make sure the cartridge is completely dead before you throw it away so you won't waste any time or money.

Using these tips can help you get the most life out of your electronic cigarette cartridge and achieve maximum usage. However, when you do need to replace your cartridge, don't just throw the old one in the trash; you should consider recycling. Throughout the United States, there are over 30,000 drop-off locations so you can recycle your cartridge, helping the environment at the same time.

BATTERIES

Since pre-filled cartridges are just disposed of, and no maintenance is required, you may not think there is much to do. However, batteries are something that can be reused and they need caring for in order to have a great effect on your electronic cigarette and help it to last longer.

As with reusable cartridges, dirt and residue can accumulate where the battery and cartridge meet. So it is a good idea to clean it with a damp cotton swab at least once a week or so in order to improve the connection between the two parts of the electronic cigarette and increase the device's performance. If the grime is allowed to harden and it doesn't come off easily, then you can use something pointy like tweezers or a toothpick to scrape out the crevasses first.

Some experience vapor smokers have suggested using a cotton swab soaked in rubbing alcohol before you wipe down the battery. However, you shouldn't do this unless you make sure it is approved by the electronic cigarette's manufacturer first. Whether you are cleaning with water or rubbing alcohol, make sure the battery is completely dry before you try to reuse it. In addition to proper cleaning, you can use the seven tips discussed earlier to help you extend the life of the battery in your electronic cigarette.

11. Accessories to Protect your Electronic Cigarette

Cleaning is the best way to fix a device that is starting to show signs of weakened vapor output, but you also need to consider ways to prevent your electronic cigarette from getting dirty or damaged in the first place. To help increase the lifespan of your device, there are an excellent number of accessories to choose from that can help protect your device from unnecessary wear and tear. Consider just a few of them.

Portable Charging Cases - With the Portable Charging Case (PCC), you can both safely store your electronic cigarettes while also carrying them around in your pocket or purse while charging them. Not only are you protecting your device from being crushed or picking up dirt, but you are also helping its ability to hold a charge.

Power Cig - If you are going to be in one place and vaping continuously then you can use this device to power your electronic cigarette from any USB port. This way you can save your batteries for when you are on the go and not unnecessarily waste your batteries.

UNIVERSAL CARRYING CASE - These sleek, pocket-sized metal carrying cases will protect your electronic cigarette and supplies. They have enough room for an electronic cigarette, two refill cartridges, and a USB charger.

LANYARD - If you want to keep your electronic cigarette close, but not in your pocket then try the vapor smoking lanyard. This securely fastens the device to your neck and allows it to be close by for easy vaping.

Before you start using any of these tips to clean your electronic cigarette, here is a word of caution. These tips are just a general guideline for what you can do to increase the lifespan of your two-piece device. It is best that you check with the manufacturer specifications before you do any kind of cleaning or maintenance. You can also ask experienced vapor smokers about what they do to extend the life of their device in order to make sure you are taking the proper steps to cleaning and maintaining your device. Otherwise, you may be doing something you think is helping, but is actually ruining your device.

12. Finding the Best Electronic Cigarette

As you have likely suspected after hearing my discussion above, the best electronic cigarette to buy depends largely on the individuals vaping needs. The everyday smoker is best suited for a rechargeable or disposable model, considering they are reasonably priced and widely accessible in recent years. On the other hand, heavy smokers may want to think about buying an electronic cigarette mod since they offer a greater level of personalization and longer lasting battery life. It is best to test out a few distinct models if possible so that you can have a greater idea of which type of model you like the most. The everyday vapers will also find an advantage to buying a back up electronic cigarette. While this doesn't necessarily have to be at the top of your list, having an extra gadget to carry you over if your main one stops working for any reason is always a good idea.

Smokeless electronic cigarettes are rapidly growing in popularity. Scientific analysis has shown that they help smokers to decrease their tobacco consumption or even to quit smoking entirely. Some studies have even shown that vapor cigarettes have helped most pack a day smokers to turn down regular smokes are just three months.

E– JUICE AND E–LIQUID

Until just a few years ago most all e-liquid came directly

from China, and a few US companies just repackaged them and sold as U.S. made. But that is no longer the case. Most e-liquids you find locally are often U.S. made. Why is that a good thing? Well, at least this way you know the ingredients they are using is real. Most e-liquids have two main ingredients, vegetable glycerin (VG) and propylene glycol(PG). Both of which can be easily found in most drug stores. If you haven't read the books I wrote on how to make your own e-liquid then, by all means, do so, and you will be amazed as to how easy it is to make your own e-liquid.

But if you are the type who doesn't want to get into the hassle of making your own e-liquid, then shop at one of the hundreds of online e-liquid stores, and you may find yourself confused with the varieties of flavors they offer, some of which are truly great tasting.

As for e-liquid, I learned one thing, not everyone likes the same flavor or type of liquids, as there are hundreds of flavors, color, and nicotine strength so everyone can try and find a few that truly suits their own taste bud.

In my first e-liquid book "How to make the Best tasting e-Liquid Ever, E-juice Recipes and Cookbook", I even shared how to make your own nicotine from Tobacco leaf organically, which has been a very popular practice now. So yes there are organic e-liquids out there that you can buy and try, but my advice would be not to get hung up with the work Organic when it comes your vaping choice, instead try to find a brand, and flavor that is well balanced (Vg/PG) and that taste great, not too dark in color as darker color liquids can damage your atomizers faster than any clear ones.

E-juices can have nicotine and it can range in amount from zero to as high as 36 MG. As I used to smoke Marlboro light cigarettes for years, for me the best suitable nicotine strength has been e-liquids with 12mg nicotine. So if you are full flavor smoker, you can try 18mg to 24mg of nicotine, but be very cautious as that maybe just little too strong for you at first. On the other hand if you smoked ultra light type cigarettes then you may want to go with 6mg nicotine strength as that is the closest to ultra light taste.

E-liquids come in a wide range of flavors depending on the different brands that are available on the market. All e-liquids contain Propylene-Glycol (PG) and/or Vegetable Glycerin (VG). There are the materials that help to create the vapor. A strong e-liquid mixture will frequently offer a vape with a powerful sensation, similar to that of inhaling cigarette smoke.

A fascinating trend is that because of the flavors and opportunity to have zero nicotine juice, even those who do not usually smoke have started to take up the vaping habit when out with friends. Between the analog cigarette changes and the new electronic nicotine delivery system users, the market is growing quickly. Vapor cigarette sales have reached over three billion dollars last year. This is considered a healthy sales statistic by most, but is also bringing some health concerns as well.

BRAND AND STYLE CHOICES

Consider just a few starter brand kit options:

- blu - $12.80 to $79.95

- V2 - $29.99 to $181.49

- Clearette - $14.99 to $299.99

- Joyetech - $59.99 to $129.99

But don't limit yourself to just these few brands, if you want to try and see what may work for you, visit a local vape shop and look at few of their devices, see what feels better in your hands, ask a lot of questions, ask them to let you try a few and then make decision based on what feels the best and has a good price.

These devices are developed in all three styles of electronic cigarettes. With so many options and price ranges to choose from it is easy to find the right starter kit for your needs.

DISPOSABLE OPTIONS

These are the gadgets most think of when it comes to envisioning an electronic cigarette. They look similar to a normal tobacco cigarette and even light up at the end so they give the appearance of traditional smoking. They often have an automatic power unit that enables when the electronic cigarette is used. Since most of these devices are small in size, they have a relatively short battery life. They often use pre-filled cartridges which are thrown out when the liquid is empty. You then have to buy additional cartridges that are specific to the device.

Refillable Options

If you are a new user looking for a more budget-cost option with strong vapor power and a long-lasting battery, then you may want to consider a refillable electronic cigarette. These devices are re-filled with e-juice that comes in a variety of flavors that can be purchased individually from a wide range of suppliers. They operate on a vapor-puff system that can be re-filled many times before having to be replaced. They have a larger battery which means they have a higher capacity and require less often recharging.

Variable Voltage / Re-Buildable Devices

If you want maximum performance and vapor achievement, then you should consider a mod or a variable voltage device. These devices offer the user a wide range of advanced features but often cost more than other models. A wide selection of vapor systems can be puffed including re-buildable atomizers that can be altered and substituted by the user. These devices are often best for the experienced electronic cigarette users who have a good understanding of how electronic cigarettes function and aspire to achieve the best possible performance that a battery powered unit can offer.

Electronic nicotine delivery systems develop a vapor that can simulate the experience of smoking when a user inhales from an electronic cigarette. There are three important parts to any electronic cigarette: a lithium power unit for powering and recharging the electronic device, an atomizer that includes the heat-up gadget which produces the vapor and a cartridge or tank that carries the e-juice liquid.

CHOOSING THE RIGHT DEVICE

There are a few options you need to research before you choose your ideal electronic cigarette:

VAPOR QUALITY

The quantity and quality of the vapor that an electronic cigarette can produce determines how well it reproduces the experience of smoking tobacco. The vapor device and the power of the battery are key factors for the quality of a device.

Disposable Electronic Cigarettes: These utilize a cartomizer system and a small power unit with low to medium vapor.

Refillable Electronic Cigarettes: These utilize a cartomizer / clearomizer with an eGo manual power unit with medium to high vapor.

Variable Voltage / Re-Buildable Electronic Cigarettes: These utilize a high voltage power unit with an improved vapor system to create very high vapor.

EASE OF USE

The clarity of a gadget in another thing to consider along with performance. An automatic battery with pre-filled cartridges is the easiest to use. A re-fillable device will require some fundamental understanding of how to refill and maintain the device in operating condition, but it will give you better capacity and is a more economical option.

Disposable Cartomizer: This is the simplest system to use. You simply screw in the cartridge and draw on the vapor cigarette to activate it.

Refillable Clearomizer: Refilling most devices in an easy process involving opening the clearomizer and placing in the e-liquid of your choice.

Variable Voltage / Re-Buildable: For these devices, you need to have a comprehension of resistance and power along with a technical knowledge of the interior workings of the device. These are recommended for knowledgeable vapers only.

REFILL AND DELIVERY SYSTEM

There are a number of systems that you can use to produce the vapor in an electronic cigarette. All of these systems have their own ups and downs, including vapor strength, flavor and the simplicity of filling. For low-cost usage, your best choice is refillable devices.

Prefilled Cartomizers: These come ready to use and are mostly not refillable. The vapor offering is limited.

Refillable Clearomizers: These have a nice offering of vapor and flavor. They are easy to use and fill.

Refillable Cartomizer-Tanks: These have a large volume and a nice vapor offering, but are more difficult when it comes to assembling and filling.

SIZE AND BATTERY LIFE

The largest part of an electronic cigarette that you need to research and consider is the size of the battery or power unit. A bigger battery will hold more charge and will have a longer lasting life. A more close-packed device with a smaller power unit is easier to transport and more discreet, but will require more frequent recharging.

Disposable Electronic Cigarettes with a Slim Automatic Battery: These are tiny and compact. The continuous time of use is two to three hours.

Refillable Electronic Cigarette with a 650mAh eGo Manual Battery: These are a rather wider gadget that will comfortably fit in a pocket. The continuous time of use is four to six hours.

Replaceable Power Unit for a Variable Voltage Mod: These utilize a wider, replaceable battery. The continuous time of use is eight to ten hours.

FLAVORS

Pre-filled cartridges offer a wide-range of flavors based on the manufacturer. When you use a refillable system, you can choose from a variety of e-liquid from many different brands. There are hundreds of distinct flavors to try, and personal likings can vary greatly.

Tobacco: For those newer to vaping, you might want to start with a traditional flavor that replicates the traditional smokes you used to smoke.

Fruits: Some people prefer the refreshing flavor of watermelon or orange or any other fruit. These can be enjoyed any time of the year when you choose your desired e-liquid fruit flavor.

Menthol Sensation: This flavor offers a crispy cool and vaguely sweet flavor that makes the sensation of menthol. Some consider this one of the best tastes available.

In my wholesale business, I carry a wide range of U.S. made e-liquids, and I have noticed over the years few flavors always sold much more than any other flavors. The top selling five flavors are:

- Watermelon
- Cotton Candy
- Peach
- Tobacco

- Pina colada

APPEARANCE

In today's world, some key elements you also need to consider are appearance and style. There is a wide range of distinct looking products available for your vaping experience. There are those that look similar in design to traditional tobacco cigarettes, or there are larger ones that have a more advanced vaping system.

Vaping is becoming a big deal in the smoking world, and electronic cigarettes are making their presence ever more known as more traditional tobacco smokers are finally making the switch over to electronic smoking.

However, the electronic cigarette market is still in its early days, and many unknowing consumers are at risk of being taken advantage of by less popular electronic brands, system, and e-liquids.

13. 10 POINTS TO CONSIDER TO HELP YOU IN YOUR BUYING PROCESS

While some of these areas have been touched on earlier, let's recap the top ten things to consider when it comes to purchasing electronic cigarettes to make sure you get the best possible device. Here is what to look for and what to avoid when purchasing your first electronic cigarette:

1. **ELECTRONIC CIGARETTE SIZE** - When it comes to

electronic cigarettes, size is an important factor. These are literally hundreds of different electronic cigarettes to choose from on the market today and just as many shapes. However, there are two main categories that you can choose from when it comes to the majority of electronic cigarettes. These are compact and full size. While most electronic cigarette devices can be interchanged or modified to operate in different ways, it is most common for compact electronic cigarettes to run off cartridges and for full-size electronic cigarettes to run off a tank system. If a small or sleek size is important for when you are in public, then it is best to consider a compact or hybrid electronic cigarette system since it is about the same size as a traditional cigarette.

2. **BATTERY LIFE** - The biggest x-factor in the world of

electronic cigarettes is the battery life. Just like cell phones took a few years to develop reliable and long lasting batteries in a small unit; it seems as though electronic cigarettes are following the same course. Most compact electronic cigarettes have a rather short battery life. So if a compact and sleek design isn't that important to you, it is a good idea to consider using a tank system or even a mod system so that you can get a good battery life.

3. **E-LIQUID TASTE** - When it comes to electronic cigarettes one of the biggest misconceptions out there is that all of them taste fruity or that they can't adequately mimic the taste of traditional tobacco. While it is true that electronic cigarettes are different from traditional cigarettes; they are pretty good at providing adequate flavor. Not only do you get a cleaner and fresher flavor with electronic smoking, but you also have a wide range of good flavors available to match any taste imaginable. Take the time to try out the different flavors available and find one that matches your palate.

4. **PRICE** - With so many systems available on the market today, it's hard for newcomers to know what a fair price is. While e-liquid itself is generally all priced the same, the systems themselves can vary greatly. You won't be surprised to find a system that can easily sell for over $200. However, if you are new to vaping it is a good idea to never pay more than $100 for a quality electronic cigarette system when you

first start. There are some systems with new and innovative technology that can be worth more than $100, but for newbies to the electronic cigarette world it is best to go with a quality, basic system first until you know what you are getting into.

5. **BATTERY CHARGE TIME** - As we have already discussed,

when it comes to electronic cigarettes the biggest thing to consider is the batteries. While battery life duration is important, it is equally important to consider the charge time when choosing which electronic cigarette system is right for you. No one has the ideal schedule or the time to charge an electronic cigarette when you forgot to plug it in before. Therefore, the general rule of thumb that most experienced vapers will tell you is that that bigger the battery the longer it will take to fully charge. So keep this in mind when deciding what system works best for your lifestyle and schedule.

6. **DURABILITY** - There are many good things about

electronic cigarettes. However, they can also be viewed as yet another electronic device you have to take care of. All of us have dealt with cell phones enough to know we don't want another flimsy electronic to worry about breaking when it hits the pavement as we get out of the car. When it comes to electronic cigarette durability, it is pretty obvious that you want to be careful not to drop the tank itself since they are often make from glass or plastic that can be broken pretty easily. However, if you are truly concerned about durability, then you may want to consider a compact electronic cigarette since they are 100% drop proof.

7. **EASE OF USE** - This is an important one for those new to

vaping. You may want to start with something that is similar to traditional smoking until you get used to the market and what's available to you. Eventually, you can graduate to a hybrid or tank system to get a more efficient vape. You don't want to start off with a difficult system and find yourself fumbling around trying to get everything right; this could end up costing you a lot in wasted supplies.

8. **E-LIQUID FLAVOR CONSISTENCY** - The e-liquid is an

important part of the electronic cigarette system. A lot of e-liquid is imported into the United States from China. The problem is that most of this are of low quality. This means you can get the inconsistent flavor, not enough vapor and sometimes not enough nicotine punch to satisfy cravings. Therefore it is important to find a quality e-liquid that allows you to notice the flavor.

9. **OVERALL SIMPLICITY** - When you are new to electronic

cigarettes, you need a system that is easy to use. There are too many devices being sold both online and in retail stores that are too complex and unnecessarily difficult for the average newcomer. Again, for newcomers it is a good idea to start with a simple, compact design until you are comfortable upgrading to a more difficult device.

10. BRAND WEBSITE SIMPLICITY AND NAVIGATION - Lastly,

this is an area most tend to overlook. Electronic cigarette is a booming market, and websites are popping up all over the place. However, most of these websites are poorly designed and don't take the user into consideration. Most of the websites are only promoting imports from China which, as discussed above, may not be the best solution. Therefore, when choosing your first electronic cigarette system make sure you know the brand and company you are purchasing from. Make sure you understand the website and have a good experience with the company when making your final decision.

14. Where to Buy

As of lately, there are hundreds of online stores that offer a great selection of branded and clone devices. Also depending on where you live, I am sure you may see a few vape shops around you. Typically online stores are cheaper than the local retailers. But if you are just starting out, don't buy anything online at first, instead visit a couple of the local vape shops, this way you can see them in person, feel them in your hands, and even try them before you actually buy any of them.

When it comes to internet and retail sales, the electronic cigarette that seems to lead the pack is the V2 Cigs or Vapour2 Cigarettes. This brand has grown from a small company to one of the most popular and top rated brands on the market today that are considered the best of the U.S. manufacturers, but some of the older Chinese brands like Innokin, Joyetech and others are still the top brands when it comes to e-cigarettes

The starter V2 kit is really an ideal option if you want to get everything in a single order at a reasonable price. Even if you are a strong traditional tobacco smoker, the starter kit will keep you going for a while without having to reorder cartridges. The kit typically comes with three V2 accumulators, twenty-five V2 flavor capsules, one AC adapter, one smart charger, one car adapter, one transportable charging case, one V2 Power Cig, one metal supporting case, one lanyard, and a comprehensive instruction manual. This is enough to get anyone started, and as we've discussed before, it has all the right accessories to help you get a handle on electronic smoking and find what works best for you.

So take the time to carefully consider what works best for your needs and eventually you will become an experienced vaper. Then you can start experimenting with a variety of flavors, vapor, and styles.

For a list, an updated list of reputable online retailers both for e-liquid and for kits, visit my blog at http://BestElectronicCigarettehq.com

Happy Vaping!~

CPSIA information can be obtained
at www.ICGtesting.com
Printed in the USA
LVHW080959270619
622533LV00016B/236/P